Give God the Glory

A Life in Grace and Goodness

Carolyn L. Smith

3G Publishing, Inc.
Loganville, Ga 30052
www.3gpublishinginc.com
Phone: 1-888-442-9637

©2020, Carolyn L. Smith. All rights reserved.

No part of this book may be reproduced, stored in a retrieval system, or transmitted by any means without the written permission of the author.

First published by 3G Publishing, Inc. February, 2022

ISBN: 9781941247884

Printed in the United States of America

Because of the dynamic nature of the Internet, any web addresses or links contained in this book may have changed since publication and may no longer be valid. The views expressed in this work are solely those of the author and do not necessarily reflect the views of the publisher, and the publisher hereby disclaims any responsibility for them.

Biblical references are from King James Version (KJV), public domain.

First Edition

Contents

Foreword – Ramona H. Pearson, CPA, MBA, CRPC 5

Introduction 11

Chapter 1 – The Title of First 15

Chapter 2 – Embracing My Story 23

Chapter 3 – Happiness and Union 35

Chapter 4 – There is a Plan 45

Chapter 5 – New Beginnings Give Life 55

Chapter 6 – The Power of Prayer 63

Notes 69

About the Author 71

Foreword

This is more than a rags to riches story. More than a story of a Big 8 Certified Public Accounting (CPA) firm Black Partner. More than a Black woman of many firsts created by a society that kept so many other deserving folks, long gone, from being the first. More than a story about semi-single parenting and marriage or not. More than family dynamics in a culture that keeps its foot on the necks and coattails of those with color. More than a story about busting through glass ceilings while keeping marriage and family and friends. More than a story about the dicey environments of Big American business and government. More than a story about the pleasurable sights of the 7 continents. More than a story about an individual.

I have known Carolyn L. Smith for almost 50 years. And, writing a foreword for her first book during the celebration of African American History could not have been a more appropriate time because I know that the history of Americans of

African descent with color in their flesh is best told through the eyes of our individual stories. But this is not just a story of a "life well lived" nor how great the person is; rather, it, as the author states, is a "focus on life as a reflection of Christ, Scripture and honoring of Truth." How wonderful it is, as well, that this book finds itself available to readers just in time for the Christian practice of Lent. The purpose of Lent isn't to "better" your life, but to re-center your life on what matters most: the One who made you and died for you. So this is not an "I" story. It IS a testimony of how the grace of God and God's presence through EVERYTHING created a story of life well lived!

Withdraw from the busyness of life and go with Carolyn L. Smith through the beginnings of life without a silver spoon on the east coast of America where from 1916 to 1970 over 6 million African Americans moved from the rural Southern United States to the urban Northeast, Midwest and West. While the joy of being away from the plantations of the South was real, the wall of Northern hatred was no less of a barrier to keeping one's sanity and hope alive..except for the knowledge that you were not alone as the author quotes Isaiah 41:10, "Fear thou not; for I am with thee: be not dismayed; for I am thy God: I will strengthen thee; yea, I will help thee; yea, I will uphold thee with the right hand of my righteousness."

Clearly Carolyn's walk with God is at the root of her being an "overcomer". So many people get "stuck" in their lives at young ages (18-30). Carolyn dusts herself off at those moments and moves forward to her commitment with the destiny God has for her. "Overcomers are followers of Christ who successfully resist the power and temptation of the world's system. An overcomer is not sinless, but holds fast to faith in Christ until the end. They do not turn away when times get difficult or become an apostate. Overcoming requires complete dependence upon God for direction, purpose, fulfillment, and strength to follow His plan for our lives (Proverbs 3:5–6; 2 Corinthians 12:9)."

In Chapter 4, Carolyn reveals the precipitous moments of a stellar career that those of us in the CPA profession know all too well. I am reminded of my first impression of Carolyn L. Smith: Wow!

Who is this beautiful, brilliant Sister! And from a Historically Black College and University (HBCU) like me! From whence cometh this amazing confidence? She is so commanding. Principled. Focused. One cat and one toy poodle, two daughters, a husband, nice amazing home with tennis courts in front! The American Dream for real! To catch her gaze was like looking into an eagle's eyes. David McNally, in the book, *"Even Eagles Need A Push"*, writes: "Confident people have a philosophy about why they were created. They have a sense of purpose, a belief that they are important, that their lives matter. Confident people know what they bring to the world. They are aware of what they are good at, their special abilities. They know that success, satisfaction, and fulfillment are the rewards for contributing their gifts and talents toward something that makes a difference." This definitely describes the person I met almost 50 years ago. However, all of that confidence was not so much in what she could do; rather, she lives Ephesians 2:10, "For we are God's handiwork, created in Christ Jesus to do good works, which God prepared in advance for us to do."

As an onlooker, when Carolyn announced her retirement, I thought (knowing the schedule and life of most then Big-8 firm partners), "Great! Her trip around the world was about to begin (Of course she had by then visited most of the continents on the planet). However, at her retirement party, Carolyn announced (in her matter-of-factly-way) that divinity school was her next stop. It drew mixed reviews in my heart as I noticed the saddened faces of her children. Yet, today, looking backward, I realize that a lifetime of preparation for what can only be described as "Evangelism" has been under God's careful guidance. Her life, *"Give God the Glory"*, is an evangelical testimony or personal witness, to spread the Christian gospel. A result of the divinity school experience and full-time evangelism opened opportunities to connect with her daughters in ways and with extended time that could not have occurred but for Carolyn's obedience to God's plan for her life.

Enjoy this journey with Carolyn and the Lord, God Almighty!

Introduction

"We are secure, not because we hold tightly to Jesus, but because He holds tightly to us."

-R.C. Sproul, theologian, writer, pastor

In Hebrews, "Give Glory to God" is an idiom meaning, "Confess your sins" [1]. The phrase compels us to speak the truth and in doing so, we honor the Creator. So, what is truth? Truth is a self-expression of God.

Jesus saith unto him, I am the way, the truth, and the life. (John 14:6)

Therefore, truth is defined by God. His eternal glory captures who He is; *Who being the brightness of his glory, and the express image of his person, and upholding all things by the word of his power, when he had by himself purged our sins, sat down on the right hand of the Majesty on high:* (Hebrews 1:3, KJV)

We bring glory to God when we honor the truth of His existence. Repeatedly in Scripture we see *honor* as a reflection of value. There is the honor done by Christ to the Father in John 8:49—*Jesus answered, I have not a devil; but I honour my Father, and ye do dishonour Me.* Paul and his companions were honored by the Melita community in Acts 28:10—*Who also honoured us with many honours; and when we departed, they laded us with such things as were necessary.* And, as we take note in Matthews 15:4, children are addressed—*For God commanded, saying, Honour thy father and mother: and, He that curseth father or mother, let him die the death.* In each of these Scriptures, and others throughout the Bible, honor is an expression of valuing that comes at a price [2].

The value of an object can be found in the weight we give it pertaining to its importance, worth, or usefulness. In essence, the more value something or someone is perceived to have, the more respect, admiration, and appreciation we tend to have towards the thing or person. Matthews 6:21 expresses the sentiment this way; *For where your treasure is, there will your heart be also.* Wherever you place your valued possessions, there you will find your heart. Notice here that the heart follows treasure, or the valued thing. We are alerted in Proverbs 4:23 to—*Keep thy heart with all diligence; for out of it are the issues of life.* I believe this is a reminder to keep the main thing in life, the main thing. That is, to focus on life as a reflection of Christ, Scripture, and honoring of Truth. This is the greatest honor you can offer the Father. To give glory is to value the price that was paid for sin so much so, that there is a willingness to follow the One who pricelessly valued your life before you were even conceived.

My journey in scribing this book begins with my desire to reflect the value of Christ in my life. As I recount the many ups and downs along my path, I am convinced that the hand of God has navigated every twist, turn, and triumph. So, this is my acknowledgement to grapple with the putting aside of my own righteousness and proclaim that all I am and all I have accomplished is in Him, the Father, the Son and the Holy Spirit. I give God the glory, for He has given me grace and goodness.

It is my hope that as you thumb through these pages, you self-reflect. How has God shown His hands in your life? What do you know for sure as a result of His grace? How has goodness and mercy followed you? I invite you to walk with me as I recount pieces of my personal life journey and discuss Scripture that shines light on the presence of Truth. To guide your introspection, at the end of each chapter you are encouraged to pause and consider your own personal relationship with the Trinity. Take your time. How you expend time reflects what you value. Honor God by giving Him your undivided attention. There are great rewards in this level of honor.

My best to you as you continue to *Give God the Glory*, Carolyn

Chapter 1

The Title of First

"The beauty of any first time is that it leads to a thousand others..."

-Pico Iyer, British-born essayist and novelist

When I initially thought about writing this book, it was to share my life story and highlight the many titles of *first* I accumulated throughout my life. As you continue to follow along, you will read about several opportunities I snared to become the *first* at accomplishing a milestone—whether planned or unplanned—through the sheer grace of God. After all, Ephesians 2:8-9 tells us, *For by grace are ye saved through faith; and that not of yourselves: it is the gift of God; Not of works, lest any man should boast.* Though the book's goal has evolved since my initial thoughts, I do want to take a moment to talk about the principle of *first* because it has been an integral part of how I have experienced God's grace and goodness in my life.

According to numerology, every number has meaning. Numeral one is characterized as upright, strong, and purposeful. Some say the number one represents strength, determination, and independence. Though I do not subscribe to any form of mystical ideology, there are many factions of my life that align to the principles of *first* and the characteristics of the number one. Over the years, life has happened to me just as it has happened to anyone who has experienced life as long as I have. But, through it all, several factors have been consistent and present, no matter the challenges or triumphs.

Life for me *"has been no crystal stair"* but it has been rewarding—with exuberant excitement sprinkled in the mix. I've always had a propensity to pick myself up, brush the dust off, and continue progressing. In hard times, I kept the words of Isaiah 41:10 close to my heart —*Fear thou not; for I am with thee: be not dismayed; for I am thy God: I will strengthen thee; yea, I will help thee; yea, I will uphold thee with the right hand of my righteousness.* I would like to think in God's grace there was an innate ability to draw from the wells of those who came before me. Life began to teach the meaning of resilience and the will to stretch for it at an early age. As time progressed, I was introduced to both interdependence and intra-dependence, understanding the need to lean on the wisdom of God in every step. This has led me to where I rest today.

As I reflect, there has been a gentle hand of mercy, love, compassion, and, well, abundance cast in the shadows of my life. Without a doubt, my footsteps have been ordered. There is nothing I regret, nothing left undone, nothing short of smiles and gratefulness. Ephesians 1:3 echoes this sentiment perfectly—*Blessed be the God and Father of our Lord Jesus Christ, who hath blessed us with all spiritual blessings in heavenly places in Christ.* I have indeed been blessed with a lifetime of highlights beyond my expectation. The titles of *first* did not come easily. To pave paths and go ahead of the pack, sacrifices were made. Untrodden territory can be exciting and frightening at the same time.

There are many African American hero and heroine stories of *first*. Thurgood Marshall (U.S. Supreme Court Justice-1967); Jackie Robinson (Major League Baseball, Brooklyn Dodgers-1947); Gwendolyn Brooks (Pulitzer Prize, Poetry-1950); Hattie McDaniel (Oscar Award-1940); Marian Anderson (singer at the White House-1962 and singer with Metropolitan Opera in New York-1955); Ella Fitzgerald (Female Grammy Award-1958); and Barack H. Obama (President of the United States of America-2008)—just to mention a few. I believe the traits associated with the number one are characteristics these heroes and heroines would have found to be common among them. In this regard, I am no different. There were many times I wondered what in the world was going on, or where exactly a path was leading. In moments of uncertainty, I leaned on God. Matthew 14:31 says, *And immediately Jesus stretched forth [his] hand, and caught him, and said unto him, O thou of little faith, wherefore didst thou doubt?* These doubts were further eased by experience mounted over time, and my experiences have led me through an amazing journey of firsts of my own.

- First college graduate in my family
- Number one in my graduating class (accounting)
- First African American woman to pass all parts of the CPA exam, in the first seating (District of Columbia)
- First African American woman District of Columbia Treasurer
- First African American Director of the Department of Finance and Revenue (District of Columbia)
- First African American female consulting partner at Coopers & Lybrand (D.C. prior to merger with Price Waterhouse)
- First non-profit organization to partner with the Ran Mine School for orphans with HIV/Aids (Zimbabwe, Africa)

In my case, and in that of others, we have been considered as pioneers by many— trailblazers of sorts, as we forged territory unscathed by others in our class. But, the paths were not untethered. There were many who led the way, marching, picketing, enduring shut-ins and shut-outs. I grew up during the 50s and 60s. The Civil Rights Movement was in full affect and the nation was on racial and economic edge. A change was coming, and it would take years to begin reconciliation of divides. The fight of those before me paved the way for me to integrate schools as a young girl. I carried the baton further by breaking racial barriers as I entered into the corporate world. Being among these pioneers was daunting, but I kept God at the forefront. One of God's own firsts was Moses himself. Leviticus 9:6 recounts—*And Moses said, This is the thing which the Lord commanded that ye should do: and the glory of the Lord shall appear unto you.* His courage led the way and continues to serve as inspiration.

The Biblical Influence of Number One

Few would disagree with the idea that number one is most significant in the Bible. Why is this so significant? Because Christians believe there is One God who is Father, Son, and Holy Spirit joined in a single unity. The Triune God, in uniqueness and sovereignty, is the One and only God. We can reflect on 1 Timothy 2:5 which denotes, *For there is one God, and one mediator between God and men, the man Christ Jesus.* Jesus is also a prime example of the significance of the number one in the Bible. He is the one son of God—*For God so loved the world, that he gave his only begotten Son, that whosoever believeth in him should not perish, but have everlasting life (John 3:16)*—and the first to be resurrected. Other figures throughout the Bible mirror this idea of *first*: John the Baptist preaching in the wilderness of Judaea, Noah building the ark, and Moses leading the Exodus are some of the most well-known.

The combination of God's grace and perseverance is powerful. Let the lessons of these leaders—both Biblical and historical—act as a guiding beacon for you to step forward and blaze your own trail of *firsts* in life as I did in mine. I am honored to share my story in the chapters ahead.

Chapter Two

Embracing My Story

"Owning our story and loving ourselves through that process is the bravest thing we'll ever do."

— Brené Brown, author

Achieving those "firsts" didn't happen overnight. Each milestone came to fruition along a journey strewn with highs and lows. First and foremost, I attest that the beginning of my journey was rooted in God. There is a succinct truth in John 1:1 that says, *In the beginning was the Word, and the Word was with God, and the Word was God.* He is the foundation upon which my life is built. I am blessed by all He's accomplished in me, and now I'd like to share where it all began.

As with each of us, my story truly started with my ancestors before me. There is respect and reverence owed to our predecessors whenever we reflect on our lives. Proverbs 17:6 teaches us, *Children's children are the crown of old men; and the glory of children are their fathers.* The glory for me rests in a long line of strong women.

Let's go back two generations to my grandmother, Carrie. You see, neither I nor my mother had a chance to meet my grandmother, but we know her story well. Carrie grew up in Winston-Salem, North Carolina. She eventually relocated to Boston after being invited to live with her newly married sister. Not long after arriving to the North, she met and fell in love with a man from town. A white man. Against all preconceived notions of the time, my grandmother Carrie believed in the power of her love and thought this new family would make her happy forever. She took the words of Colossians 3:14 to heart—*And above all these things put on love, which is the bond of perfectness.* The dream of a perfect family was swiftly dashed when the man refused a legal union. His rejection was too much for Carrie to bear—tragically, she ended her life by jumping into the Boston Bay. The newborn she left behind, my mother, was sent back to Winston-Salem to be raised by her grandmother.

My mother's own budding romance unfolded before her as she became a young woman. Davis, the man who would become my father, had just been released from prison after serving 20 years for murder. That didn't sway my mother. Once she and Davis crossed paths, the connection was instant. Their courtship blossomed in North Carolina, but they eventually moved their roots north to Newark, New Jersey where Davis secured a position at the local African American Newspaper. Between the pages of this love story, I was born to my parents in 1942 along with my brothers Carl and Richard who were born in 1941 and 1947, respectively. Echoing the song of my grandmother's fortune, my birth did not bring my parents together in marriage. When Davis continued to refuse a legal union, my mother decided to return to North Carolina so that we could be raised with the help of her grandmother. My mom did her part to support us by working at the Winston-Salem Teachers College. She never earned her degree and wasn't a teacher there, but she helped as an administrative assistant.

I remember my childhood in the South fondly. My great-grandmother raised chickens and pigs and tended to expansive gardens. Whenever we had a special meal, I remember her wringing a chicken's neck, dipping it into boiling hot water, and plucking out its feathers before cooking it to perfection. My siblings and I helped by picking a few vegetables from the garden nearby. It wasn't all idyllic though. When I was five years old I came down with rheumatic fever, fighting for my life in the hospital over six hard months. By the grace of God and the power of prayer, I pulled through to the other side and became healthy again. James 5:15 says, *And the prayer of faith shall save the sick, and the Lord shall raise him up.* It is true, faithful prayer is often underestimated. I had my family and community surrounding me with well wishes that aided my healing. As soon as I was well again, my mother decided to leave the shroud of sickness behind us and move our family to Washington, D.C.

The city of D.C. was lively, bustling, and coursing with energy—a far cry from the country roads of my great-grandmother's house, to say the least. Now the place we called home was a rooming house on 2nd Street Northwest, just below Howard University. I went to elementary school at Mott Elementary School. My mom transitioned from being an administrative assistant to a nursing home assistant, and we lived a comfortable life.

When I was still in elementary school we moved to a new rooming house in the 1300 block of G Street N.E. I was transferred to Lovejoy Elementary School.

Some Sundays we gathered as a family and went down to a Baptist church on the corner of 13th Street and G Street Northeast. One morning among the pews, the Lord picked my heart to join the church. That was a defining moment for me, and I started going to church on a regular basis. As portrayed by Deuteronomy 13:4, I gave my life to the Lord—*Ye shall walk after the Lord your God, and fear him, and keep his commandments, and obey his voice, and ye shall serve him, and cleave unto him.* God has always been in my life, but from that moment I entered a new level of intentionality that came with joining a church family.

My mother's second chance at love came along when we moved to a new, larger rooming house in North East. There she met William—he lived on the first floor, while we lived on the second floor. He started as a friendly neighbor, and with time became increasingly intertwined into our lives. He formed a bond not only with my mother but also with me and my siblings. Before my mother and stepfather were married, my mother became ill and had to be hospitalized for surgery. My two brothers and I were placed in the district's orphanage, D.C. Village, until mom was discharged. We only had to stay in the orphanage a week. As soon as my mother was released from the hospital at the end of a week. She began taking care of us again. She was a loving mother to all of her children all of her life and we returned her love.

My mother received government welfare checks until she was able to return to work. The time I spent away from my mother was dark and troubling since we did not know how long we would be in the orphanage. I prayed and remembered Psalm 23:4— *Yea, though I walk through the valley of the shadow of death, I will fear no evil: for thou art with me; thy rod and thy staff they comfort me.* With these words I remained strong for my siblings and kept faith that we would all be reunited again.

God's grace shined through anew, and my mother became well again. I don't remember her illness exactly; but whatever it was, she overcame it and lived until two months shy of her 88th birthday.

Once she was able to return to work, she brought us out of the orphanage and back home to be with the family. *Behold, how good and how pleasant it is for brethren to dwell together in unity! (Psalm 133:1).*

She and William continued to date. Before marriage she was pregnant with my brother George and gave birth in 1951. William joined our family as our stepfather when he and my mother married in 1952; my new little brother Billy followed shortly after, born in 1953. We were quite the happy family. My parents supported us by managing an apartment building and driving taxicabs, and we attended school around the corner at Logan Elementary School.

Later when I entered junior high school, I was bused across town. Even though there was a school across the street from where I lived, I could not attend because of segregation. When integration was declared in D.C. I transferred to Stuart Junior High School, located across the street.

We later moved to the outskirts of D.C. after my eighth-grade school year. We settled into the town of Norbeck in Montgomery County, Maryland. Our property in Norbeck had a couple acres of land where we raised chickens and pigs and sold eggs. It almost felt like we were back at my great-grandmother's home down south. We didn't have indoor plumbing, so we kept a tin tub in the kitchen to bathe. Back then, a bath was no simple feat. First, we pumped water from the well out back. Then we heated the water to a decent temperature and filled that tin tub. Since I was the only girl, I always had the privilege of taking the first bath. The boys would go after me from youngest to oldest—same tub, same bathwater. We had an outhouse up the hill, too. To avoid going outside at night, we kept a "porta potty" of sorts in the house that we emptied every day before going to school. It wasn't a life of luxury, but I was grateful to God to have my family together. I didn't take it for granted and embraced the sentiment of Deuteronomy 26:11—*And thou shalt rejoice in every good thing which the Lord thy God hath given unto thee.*

Schools were still segregated back in those days in Maryland, but things began to change as I entered ninth grade. At first I rode the bus a few towns over to Rockville where I attended Lincoln Junior High for black students. Then, at the cusp of racial integration, I was transferred to Sherwood Middle and High school nearby. I was the very first black person to be a part of that student body, and everyone there made sure I knew it. I remember sitting in the cafeteria at lunch and feeling utterly alone. My white classmates' treatment of me could only be described as evil and nasty. They called me names and said I didn't belong there. They shouted at me to go back where I came from. Even worse, the adults made no effort to halt the poor behavior I faced. In the midst of those times feeling separate and singled out, I would remember the words of Isaiah 41:10—*So do not fear, for I am with you; do not be dismayed, for I am your God. I will strengthen you and help you; I will uphold you with my righteous right hand.* It wasn't easy, but with God by my side I stood up proudly and persevered.

After being in Maryland for three or four years, my parents decided to move back to D.C. I was a junior then and enrolled in McKinley Technical High School, which was already integrated. The teachers insisted I wasn't college-bound material, so they placed me in what were called track three classes. Back then, the district had four tracks—track three and four students were definitely not going to college. Instead, teachers encouraged us to seek a good government job as a clerk or some similar position. I decided early on in high school that I was going to college regardless of what my teachers drilled into my head or what track they put me on. I told my two best friends, who were also in track three classes, that I was not getting a government job. I was going to college. The three of us worked diligently, and contrary to our teachers' bidding, we were all accepted into Howard University and earned college degrees. We didn't let our circumstances hold us back, for as Philippians 4:13 says, *I can do all things through Christ which strengtheneth me.* The negativity of our teachers was drowned out by our faith and determination.

Decades later, the three of us still stick together. We remained close friends throughout high school and college, and one was even a bridesmaid in my wedding. It's hard to believe that in 2020 we celebrated our 60th anniversary of graduating from high school. I've achieved so many more dreams in my life since that time but will always remember the beginnings I faced with my family, friends, and God by my side.

Chapter Three

Happiness and Union

"Happiness is not something you postpone for the future; it is something you design for the present."

-Jim Rohn, American businessman

When I first arrived at Howard University, the campus was buzzing with excitement and possibility. Everyone had a dream they were rushing towards; the passion in the air was palpable and contagious. In that first semester, I had my sights set on becoming a history teacher. I could see myself at the front of a classroom, wisely passing down knowledge to the next generation. The idea quickly crumbled when I received my first report card with a giant, glaring "F" in none other than History 101.

That failure knocked me down for a moment, but I jumped right back on the horse and decided to go for another subject. Make no mistake—picking yourself up after a setback is no easy task, but I've found there's power in pushing through and trying again. We can learn this in Romans 5:3-5—*And not only so, but we glory in tribulations also: knowing that tribulation worketh patience; and patience, experience; and experience, hope: And hope maketh not ashamed; because the love of God is shed abroad in our hearts by the Holy Ghost which is given unto us.* That's to say, the triumph and fruit of our struggles is the grit we gain from getting back up and finding a way to keep going. I can't tell you how many majors I tried—political science, communications, social work, and English, to name a few. At the end of the day, none of them lit a spark but I had hope for finding my niche.

Amid this ongoing pursuit, I was working tirelessly to keep myself enrolled in the first place. I got a job working in Lerner Shops as a cashier to pay my way since my parents couldn't afford the tuition and I didn't get a scholarship. I remember when I got a pay raise earning 90 cents an hour. I thought I was going to be rich! That was enough for me to make use of an old car my father gave me so I could drive myself back and forth between work and school.

Eventually I reached a point where I was trying to choose yet another major to pursue. There were so many failed subjects piling up behind me, and I felt that I was at the end of my rope. That's when my friend Bernard stepped in with an idea. Bernard and I met at Howard and really enjoyed each other's company. We dated for a short time, but it always felt like a friendship more than a romance. While I was working at the Learner Shop one day, he stopped by to visit and suggested I give majoring in accounting a shot. I had no clue what the subject was about at all. He explained the general idea to me, and I decided to give it a try. After going through so many other majors, what did I have to lose? It turns out accounting was exactly what I was looking for and what God had in store for me. After five years, I graduated at the top of my class in accounting.

Bernard was a great friend to me, and I'll always appreciate his help, but the feelings I had for him never grew to be more than platonic. In a way, his guidance toward the path of accounting led me to the person I would marry. It all happened during the last accounting course of my last semester. I was sitting in my chair, focused and in the zone; I could almost imagine how it would feel to walk across the stage in just a few months. Out of nowhere I felt a slight tug on my hair, just enough to shake my concentration. I turned around ready to fuss until I saw a handsomely coy face looking back at me. His name was Vernon. We chatted after class, and I learned that he was a political science major taking accounting as an elective. We had instant chemistry and were eager to spend time together outside of our studies. After dating for some time, I had no doubt I wanted to spend the rest of my life with him. 1 John 4:17-19 says, *Herein is our love made perfect, that we may have boldness in the day of judgment: because as he is, so are we in this world. There is no fear in love; but perfect love casteth out fear: because fear hath torment. He that feareth is not made perfect in love. We love him, because he first loved us.* With no trace of fear in my heart, I took a leap of faith and asked him to marry me.

This is where the bubble began to burst. Vernon accepted my proposal on one condition: I would have to convert to Catholicism in order to marry into his faith. We hadn't talked much about religion before, but I loved and respected him enough to move forward with the idea. He suggested that I get in touch with Georgetown University, which is a Catholic school in Washington, D.C. They would guide me through three months of study and teach me the tenets of the religion so I could ultimately convert. I started the process and began planning the wedding along the way.

There were several classes I had to take at Georgetown University as I did my due diligence to prepare for life with my future husband. The three months crept by until I reached the final step towards becoming a Catholic: confessing every sin that I'd ever committed from birth to the present. I sat in a small booth within the church, wracking my brain to remember my sins. This wasn't something I was accustomed to in my Baptist upbringing, but 1 John 1:9 says, *If we confess our sins, he is faithful and just to forgive us our sins, and to cleanse us from all unrighteousness.* I would adopt the practice as the last hurdle towards Catholicism before my marriage. The priest was patiently lending an ear on the other side of the wall. When I couldn't think of a single sin to add, I told him that's as much as I could remember; take it or leave it. They accepted my confession heartily, and the process was complete. Finally!

Before I knew it, the date was October 15, 1965—the day before our wedding. All our friends and family were arriving in town from down south. Amid the final preparations, the priest called Vernon and me to come by the church. Among the overview of last details, the subject of communion came up. He told us that when the time for communion comes around, only I would take communion since Vernon's not Catholic. Everything seemed to freeze in that moment. Not Catholic? Surely he was mistaken.

All the excitement and anticipation welling up inside me twisted into a heavy knot in my stomach. I couldn't believe what I had just heard. After all this, Vernon was not Catholic. Why had he lied to me? I was completely overwhelmed and could barely process the information. The thought of postponing the wedding crossed my mind, but I decided against it. I had asked him to marry me; and he put me through all these challenges, so I wasn't stopping now. There were groomsmen and bridesmaids who rented tuxes and dresses, and relatives who traveled from far and wide. No—the wedding would not be postponed. I was somewhat in shock, but I loved him so much. I simply pushed through my feelings. In hindsight, perhaps I was overlooking his wrongs and grasping at the words of Romans 3:23—*For all have sinned and come short of the glory of God.* None of us is perfect. Despite his lie, was I clinging to the goodness I knew Vernon had within? There was some relief; however, I never truly wanted to become Catholic. There was a contrast of emotions as I was both relieved and shocked.

Our marriage carried along fine for a while. In time, however, I found that one reason Vernon wanted me to convert was to ensure that I would be faithful in our marriage. He wanted me to be faithful to him and him alone. The impact of fear and insecurity on our lives can be unrelenting. These two evils would rear their ugly heads many times throughout our union. At a certain point, I felt the scale of our relationship tip; there were long periods of loneliness and countless twists of ups and downs. However, through it all I held on to hope and the promises of God.

We weren't promised a lifetime of peace. As a matter of fact, Luke 12:51 reminds us to expect conflict on the Christian path.

"Suppose ye that I am come to give peace on earth? I tell you, Nay; but rather division."

Wherever religion or Christianity is concerned, we can anticipate divisiveness. Everyone will not become a follower of Christ, and for some who do, persecution will become a reality. Christ is clear about the distinction between his disciples and non-believers. I suspect, in this vein, Christians must be comfortable with division. When we think differently, even in minor things, there can be disagreement. And, while peace is desirable, we are called to be unwavering in convictions that align to the Word of God. Harmony is not always possible or good.

Processing the beginnings of our relationship, our marriage, and Vernon's death has weighed heavily upon me over the years. Nevertheless, my personal journey with God deviated from time to time, but he gave me the strength to continue and ultimately put His love first. We are encouraged to do this by the message portrayed in Matthews 22: 37-38—*Je-*

sus said unto him, Thou shalt love the Lord thy God with all thy heart, and with all thy soul, and with all thy mind. This is the first and great commandment.
Let us keep the Lord's love first and prosper.

Chapter Four

There is a Plan

The most important lesson that I have learned is to trust God in every circumstance. Lots of times we go through different trials and following God's plan seems like it doesn't make any sense at all. God is always in control and he will never leave us."

-Allyson Felix, American athlete

After years of hard work and a tireless journey of self-discovery, I graduated from Howard University at the top of my class with a degree in accounting. I thought the world would be my oyster, bursting with opportunities to apply my newly minted education and make a difference. However, as soon as I took a step forward, the oyster's shell snapped shut in my face.

Regardless of the strides I had made in my studies, the fact remained that I was a black woman in America. The year was 1965 and segregation was very real. I took the initiative of calling the top eight accounting firms in the DC area to inquire about open positions, being sure to tell them I was number one in my class. When they discovered my alma mater was Howard, they laughed in my face. I'll never forget when a representative from one of the firms I called said to me, "You can't be serious. We don't hire blacks, and we don't hire women." The next thing I heard was a click as he hung up the phone. I received similar responses from the other firms in the area—if not as harsh, they simply let me know they didn't have anything available "for me."

I felt so discouraged. These rejections were especially concerning because I needed to secure two years working in the field in order to be eligible to take the CPA exam. Specifically, the work had to be completed at a licensed CPA accounting firm that offered auditing and accounting. By being shut out from these firms, I was left with no ground to stand on. I reached a point where I realized that even if I didn't get the kind of job needed for the CPA exam, I had to work somewhere to survive in the meantime. After all, Romans 8:31 tells us, *What shall we then say to these things? If God be for us, who can be against us?* Even though I received these rejections, God was on my side and my journey was far from over. Eventually, I had the idea of contacting the United Planning Organization, which was a non-profit group that worked with the needy. I spoke to them about my education and goals of gaining field experience; and to my delight, they offered me a position in their accounting department. I was ecstatic! The starting salary was $6,800 a year which was pretty good back then.

After working with United Planning for a couple of years, integration in the workforce started to become more commonplace. I decided to reach out to the area's big accounting firms again, seeking opportunities to go deeper into the field. One of my first calls was to Lybrand Ross Brothers and Montgomery—they had turned me away before, but they weren't as incredibly rude as the folks over at the other firms; so I figured I'd have better luck with them. I was right. Instead of shutting me down on the spot, they agreed to have me come in as the next step of the interview process. On the morning of the interview, I dressed to the nines and did everything I could to prepare for the meeting. The experience of going into their offices rekindled the feelings I had as a young girl, walking through the halls of my newly integrated middle school. I held my own in the interview and was ultimately hired into the auditing branch of Lybrand Ross Brothers and Montgomery in 1967.

Fast forward another two years, and I had acquired enough in-field experience to take the CPA exam. I sat for the exam in May of 1969 and passed on my first try with great scores. Because of this accomplishment, Lybrand Ross Brothers and Montgomery kept me on and even promoted me to a senior auditor. I was moving along on the path towards partnership of the firm when I was happily interrupted by the birth of my first child in 1970. My career continued after two months of maternity leave, and I returned to work with the firm. Throughout these first years of being in the workforce, my husband was steadily studying at Howard and in 1973 he had the opportunity to pursue his doctorate degree at UCLA. His acceptance into the program was a rarity back in those days, so there was no question about our family making the move to California. I was worried about leaving Lybrand

Ross Brothers and Montgomery at first, but they assured me that I could transfer to their Los Angeles office to extend my position and further my roots. The arrangement was mutually beneficial—they didn't want to lose one of the few minorities they had on the docket. Everything seemed to align, and we made the jump to the West Coast.

It was during my resettling into Washington, DC in 1977 when things began to take off with my career. I had a few solid years of accounting experience behind me, not to mention a string of promotions within the firm. One of my husband's fraternity brothers who was an attorney in Washington, DC asked Vernon if I was interested in pursuing an opportunity in government. The Mayor of Washington was Walter Washington, an African American man who achieved the feat of becoming the first elected Black mayor of DC. He needed a treasurer because the previous person had just been arrested for fraud. The friend asked if I was interested in pursuing the opportunity and when I said yes, he set up the interview with Mayor Walter Washington. Next thing I knew, I was the first female African American treasurer for Washington, DC. When paths cross and plans align themselves before your feet, all you can do is acknowledge and appreciate God's work and pray that he continues to do so. This essence is reflected in Proverbs 3:6 which reads, *In all thy ways acknowledge Him, and He shall direct thy paths.*

I remained the treasurer through Walter Washington's term and was reappointed by Marion Barry when he was elected as the next mayor. Mayor Barry then appointed me to become the first black director of the Department of Finance and Revenue, handling all the District's funds. By his reelection in 1984, I decided I wanted to leave the government and go back to Lybrand Ross Brother and Montgomery. The mayor was supportive of my decision, and even reached out to the firm to warn that if I didn't get the position of partner, they wouldn't get any further business from DC government. Needless to say, I was back in business in the corporate accounting world. They hired me back as a senior manager on track to partner.

Soon after, I was approached by Mr. Larry Doss, an African American man who was a Principal in the firm. He ran the firm's government consulting practice. To clarify between the two realms, auditing is basically a numbers game analyzing the financial activity of an organization, whereas consulting is helping them manage their business. Larry and I met to discuss my work experience and background, and he offered a proposition on the spot. If I came to work in his consulting practice, he guaranteed I would earn the position of partner after a year's time. I took him up on the offer because I knew the further I delved into the private corporate world, the higher my income would be. Larry stuck to his word and I was promoted to partner of the firm in the government practice after one year. In a sad turn of events, he died shortly after my promotion. I stepped up and took over his practice as main partner at that time, becoming one of the first African American women to do so.

In the late 80s and early 90s, many of the accounting firms in the DC area began to merge. Lybrand Ross Brothers and Montgomery acquired Coopers Brother, a London firm and we became Coopers and Lybrand. Then Coopers and Lybrand later acquired Price Waterhouse in the early 1990s. We then became Price Waterhouse Coopers. I was a partner in the government practice of the merged firms in the DC office. In addition to this role, I also joined the Women's National Democratic Club on the board of their finance staff. Associating with such a distinguished group of women definitely had its benefits. While in these positions, I used the power I held to serve as a mentor to countless young and upcoming black accountants—both offering sage advice and hiring them into my firm when possible.

Looking back on my career, I am proud of all that I accomplished and strive to pass down whatever I can to the next generation. Mentorship is a powerful tool that further solidifies and validates our contributions to the world. 2 Timothy 2:2 teaches us, *And the things that thou hast heard of me among many witnesses, the same commit thou to faithful men, who shall be able to teach others also.* To this day, I still stay in touch and get support from the men and women I took under my wing. I pray they'll continue the flow of knowledge and pour their own wisdom into the next pool of young people, thereby enriching minds for years to come.

Recently I was able to connect with a few mentees in person during the National Association of Black Accountants Annual Evening with NABA Washington, DC dinner that was held in the Spring of 2019. There I was honored with their coveted lifetime achievement award. As I looked humbly into the faces of everyone applauding in the crowd, I knew deep down that God always had a plan for me. Jeremiah 29:11 says, *For I know the thoughts that I think toward you, saith the Lord, thoughts of peace, and not of evil, to give you an expected end.* This message can be seen as I look back on my life, and also shines through time and time again in the Bible. We see it in the stories of Moses and Pharaoh, Jacob and Esau, and the Parable of the Talents. The lesson is that even when times seem impossibly difficult and the path ahead is completely clouded, God is still in control.

Because of God's plan, I was fortunate enough to make a difference in this world. That realization as I accepted my award was a beautiful moment that I'll cherish for the rest of my days.

Chapter Five

New Beginnings Give Life

"Therefore if any man be in Christ, he is a new creature: old things are passed away; behold, all things are become new."

-2 Corinthians 5:17

The journey of my career was as arduous as it was rewarding. I could see my legacy living on through those I mentored over the years. After pouring so much of myself into the past few decades, it was suddenly time to leave it all behind. Price Waterhouse Coopers offered early retirement for partners in their late fifties and mandatory retirement at age sixty. Once fifty-eight years had crept up on me, it was my turn to bow out from the firm.

As the door closed on that chapter of my life, I was ready to bound into the next phase. I had it all planned out. During the winter months I would jet off to the Caribbean island of St. Thomas where my youngest daughter lived. The perfect retirement nest was waiting for me—a two-bedroom condo overlooking the ocean on one side and boasting the green backdrop of a golf course on the other. My first time to fly south came along just as the D.C. air was getting crisp. Bags were packed and the car was loaded. I sat perched on the edge of my bed, lacing up my shoes before heading out the door when something stopped me cold. It was the voice of Jesus speaking to me. As clear as day, the voice said, "I have something for you to do." I was shaken to say the least.

I boarded the plane to St. Thomas as planned but didn't unpack and settle in once I got there. Instead, I arranged to sell the condo on the spot and promptly made my way back to Washington, DC. The first thing I did when I returned was visit my pastor. I told him what I'd heard about Jesus having some purpose for me and I asked him what I should do next. After some consideration, my pastor replied that perhaps God wanted me to go to seminary. Maybe this was the "calling" that so many nuns, priests, and preachers had heard before me. He sent me to the Progressive National Baptist Convention headquartered nearby in Maryland so that I could learn more about a path forward.

Although I had been an avid churchgoer most of my life, I had no formal experience in theology and fully expected to start from the bottom in an undergraduate program. Upon speaking with members of the Progressive National Baptist Convention, I was surprised when they directed me to seminary at the master's degree level. No sooner than I started seminary, I heard God's voice again. The Lord wanted me to channel my studies into the pursuit of mission work. The significance of this work lies in the ability of a servant of Christ to lift their voice and spread His word to new communities. Matthew 28:18-20 preaches, *And Jesus came and spake unto them, saying, All power is given unto me in heaven and in earth. Go ye therefore, and teach all nations, baptizing them in the name of the Father, and of the Son, and of the Holy Ghost: Teaching them to observe all things whatsoever I have commanded you: and, lo, I am with you always, even unto the end of the world.* I couldn't have asked for a more meaningful objective, and I followed God's calling faithfully.

When my retirement party came around, I decided it was the perfect moment to announce my enrollment in seminary school with the goal to work in missions. A good friend and former co-worker named Loxley came up to me after the party and, to my surprise and delight, told me he was coming with me on the path to seminary. Loxley was one of the many young professionals I mentored during my career. I met him while he was a student at Howard University and hired him into my firm right after he graduated. I'd become somewhat of an adopted mother to him, always taking him under my wing and offering my guidance when I could. He was very adamant about his decision to attend seminary, so I ended up having a companion along this new life journey. I graduated from the seminary program before Loxley, and I guided him into the field of missions. Now he's an ordained reverend at one of the largest AME churches in the world; and we've done ministry together, spreading the good Word in his homeland of Jamaica and other places around the world.

Whether in Jamaica or elsewhere in the world, my utmost goal during this phase of my life is to be a sounding horn for God. The passage of Matthew 25:14-31 paints a picture of just how far-reaching mission work can be, both literally and figuratively. Matthew 25:14-15 opens with, *For the kingdom of heaven is as a man travelling into a far country, who called his own servants, and delivered unto them his goods. And unto one he gave five talents, to another two, and to another one; to every man according to his several abilities; and straightway took his journey.* On missions, we set out with our own "talents" comprised of God's word, His love, and the light that emanates from being joined with Him.

As we reach communities who have yet to know God, we allow that light to shine out and multiply as described in Matthew 25:16-17 — *Then he that had received the five talents went and traded with the same, and made them other five talents. And likewise, he that had received two, he also gained other two.* I may be just one person, but any connection I make helps to spread God's love in ripples that will continue to make an impact. The passage in Matthew 25 goes on to describe the servants who multiplied their talents later being rewarded for their efforts. We see this in Matthew 25:23 — *His lord said unto him, Well done, good and faithful servant; thou hast been faithful over a few things, I will make thee ruler over many things: enter thou into the joy of thy lord.* On the other hand, the servant who kept his talents hidden and did not multiply failed to receive a reward along with the others.

The lesson is that we can all take part in the endeavor of missions, whether on a large or small scale. For some of us, including myself, mission work means embarking on service trips to foreign lands. For others, it may be the simple act of treating a stranger with kindness. The important thing is for us all to continue spreading God's love throughout our journeys in life.

What is love?

Love is patient.

Love is kind.

Love does not envy.

Love does not behave rudely.

Love does not seek its own.

Love is not provoked.

Love thinks no evil.

Loves does not rejoice in iniquity.

Love rejoices in the truth.

Love bears all things.

Love believes all things.

Love hopes all things.

Love endures all things.

Love never fails.

-1 Corinthians 13:4-8

Chapter Six

The Power of Prayer

"Prayer turns ordinary mortals into men of power. It brings power. It brings fire. It brings rain. It brings life. It brings God."

-Samuel Chadwick, minister

The hand of God has been evident in my life since birth. I believe I have been covered for the purpose of doing exactly what I am doing now. During my journey I've overcome sickness, faced separation from my family, and battled the hardships of discrimination; but in the end, I persevered. Each step has been orchestrated to lead me to mission work and shepherding the poor and less fortunate. In order to remain true to that ordained path and stay in touch with God's will, I have relied fiercely on the power of prayer.

For many Christians, prayer is something taught to us from the time we are little children, reciting rhyming lines before resting our heads each night. As we grow older and become more intentional in our practice, it's important to take time to ruminate on the action of prayer itself. What is prayer at its core? I believe prayer is the channel of communication with the very source of our existence—God. It is the act of worship that raises glory to Him and reinforces our need for Him. Jeremiah 33:3 plainly says, *Call unto me, and I will answer thee, and show thee great and mighty things, which thou knowest not.* Our souls require prayer for understanding, growth, and unity with God. Prayer provided the bridge between many moments of hardship that I came across during my life.

Just as significant as the "what" is the "why." Why should we take time out of our day to pray? Of course, we can find a multitude of reasons. Prayer provides us the power to discern God's will and tap into His plan for us. It is the method for bringing our requests to the Lord's feet so that we may humbly ask for his help and guidance. Within the writings of Luke 11:9 we read, *And I say unto you,*

Ask, and it shall be given you; seek, and ye shall find; knock, and it shall be opened unto you. Because of prayer, we can draw on God's strength and find the courage to overcome our obstacles. We work together with God's power when we pray, and the practice further roots us in our values. In good times, prayer is giving recognition to the Lord that we are grateful for his role in our happiness and blessings. In my own story, I prayed just as hard when I was in the orphanage as when I was reunited with my family. Prayer is simply a way of opening up ourselves to God, which is reason enough in itself.

When we think of prayer, we often hold the idealistic notion that our desires will always be granted. This can sometimes lead to disillusion when things don't go our way. If the Bible tells us, *The righteous cry, and the Lord heareth, and delivereth them out of all their troubles (Psalms 34:17)*, then why would God intervene in some cases but not in others? As our scientific understanding of the universe has grown and times seem darker than ever, it is only natural for doubts to be sown. This is where faith comes in. Instead of viewing prayer as a black and white method for getting what is asked like a transaction at the bank, we must see it as creating an opening for God to work in our lives. It is the exercise of quieting our minds and allowing ourselves to experience God, always believing that he has a plan. Matthew 21:22 says, *And all things, whatsoever ye shall ask in prayer, believing, ye shall receive.* The key of this verse rests in believing. In moments when it seems as though our prayers are left unanswered; we must keep faith that God has heard us. I remember having this feeling early in my career when I was rejected over and over from working in a top accounting firm. I began to feel doubtful of my prayers and questioned my path, especially after all my hard work in school to reach that point. Looking back, I know it must not have been the right time and that I was meant to start out in the smaller minority organization first. I kept the faith.

Sometimes when it comes to prayer, the hardest obstacle is knowing where to start. How does one choose the right words? What if we don't sound as eloquent as the reverends in church on Sunday morning? As your mind races with all the things you want God to do for you, first take a moment to step back and give thanks for what he's already done. Perhaps it's your health, the family that surrounds you, a roof over your head, or each breath you draw—begin with a declaration of gratitude to ground the prayer and lay the foundation for your conversation with God. Philippians 4:6-7 reaffirms this when it says, *Be careful for nothing; but in every thing by prayer and supplication with thanksgiving let your requests be made known unto God. And the peace of God, which passeth all understanding, shall keep your hearts and minds through Christ Jesus.* Try starting each day with a thankful prayer, and you will find yourself more and more fulfilled through the blessings you already possess.

Before all fails, I encourage you to draw upon the building blocks of prayer as provided in the Bible—the Lord's prayer—which I've included below to close this chapter. No matter how you choose to pray, keep the Lord at the center of your mind and always give God the glory.

The LORD's Prayer

"Our Father which art in heaven, Hallowed be thy name.

Thy kingdom come, Thy will be done on earth, as it is in heaven.

Give us this day our daily bread.

And forgive us our debts, as we forgive our debtors.

And lead us not into temptation, but deliver us from evil: For thine is the kingdom, and the power, and the glory, forever. Amen."

- Matthew 6: 9-13

Notes

1 Easton's Bible Dictionary. Retrieved at https://www.blueletterbible.org/search/Dictionary/viewTopic.cfm?topic=ET0001504

2 Vine's Expository Dictionary of New Testament Words. Retrieved at https://www.blueletterbible.org/search/Dictionary/viewTopic.cfm?topic=VT0001401

The Author
Carolyn L. Smith

In May, 1969, Carolyn L. Smith became the first black female to pass the Certified Public Accountant (CPA) exam in the District of Columbia. With this accomplishment, she now had the credential deemed the differentiator in the accounting profession. But she was still a woman, a black woman. Carolyn's determination, perseverance, quest for excellence, desire to leave a lasting impact would propel her to achievements at the highest levels in the profession for over 40 years. After a successful career in the world of accounting and finance, her next purpose and passion would emerge.

Carolyn currently serves as President of the Bindura Christian Fellowship, Inc. (BCF), a 501©3 non-profit mission organization. With two of her fellow seminary graduates, she founded BCF in the fall of 2005. BCF has taken many annual mission trips to Zimbabwe, Ghana, Nigeria, Haiti, Jamaica, and many other countries. The mission trips provide teaching, evangelism and resources to support the needs of the people. The vision for BCF emerged from her early post retirement work as the Special Projects Coordinator for the Missions Ministry of the Mount Pleasant Baptist Church, Washington, D. C. In this capacity, she was responsible for coordinating mission trips. After graduating from Capital Bible Seminary in 2005, Carolyn returned to the Seminary as a volunteer teacher of Mission Services of Women.

Carolyn's career in the world of accounting and finance began in the 60's, a tough time for our nation and the world, as a whole. While she was strategic and intentional in her pursuit of professional success, Carolyn was similarly dedicated to helping others and impacting communities, while fulfilling the role of a wife and mother of two children. She was a volunteer leader in numerous organizations and a mentor to many professionals and students across the country. Prior to her retirement, Carolyn was a partner in the Washington, D.C. office of Price Waterhouse Coopers (PWC), formerly Coopers & Lybrand, LLP (Coopers), working in the Government Consulting Group serving state and local governments, higher education institutions and non-profit organizations.

Carolyn started her career working in the non-profit sector from 1965 to 1967. Also during 1967, she went to work for Lybrand Ross Bros. & Montgomery (LRB&M), one of the Big 8 CPA firms. After passing the CPA exam in 1969, she was promoted to senior auditor for LRB&M, which later became Coopers Lybrand & Ross (Coopers). In 1977, she left Coopers for an appointment as the Treasurer and later Director of the Department of Finance and Revenue for the District of Columbia. Carolyn was the first African American woman to serve in these roles. She returned to Coopers in the mid 1980's. In 1986, she was admitted to the partnership at Coopers. Carolyn was one of two African American women to be admitted to the partnership at Coopers at that time. Carolyn retired from PWC in 2001.

Carolyn's extensive volunteerism has included serving as President of the Metropolitan Washington, DC Chapter of NABA and the founder of the chapter's signature event, "Evening with NABA";

Treasurer for the District of Columbia Chamber of Commerce; Co-Chair of Government Directions Committee, DC Budget and Financial Priorities Commission; Treasurer, DC Committee to Promote Washington; Chair of the Investment Committee for the Woman's National Democratic Club; and a member of the American Institute of Certified Public Accountants. Carolyn also served as an advisor to Mayor Marion Barry on budget and financial matters.

Carolyn has been a member of Zion Church since 2007 where she serves with the evangelism ministry, and is a small group member. She formerly served monthly at the Prince Georges County Food Bank with members of the United Baptist Church in New Carrollton, MD. Currently, Carolyn participates in praise and worship services twice a month with Reverend Loxley O'Connor at the Independence Court Nursing Home in New Carrollton. MD. Carolyn has been listed in Who's Who in the East [United States], Who's Who of American Women, and Who's Who Among Black Americans.

Carolyn received a Master of Divinity and Missions from Capital Bible Seminary in May, 2005, an M.B.A. in Finance from the University of Maryland, College Park, in 1994, and a B.A. in Accounting, with a minor in Economics in 1965, from Howard University.

www.ingramcontent.com/pod-product-compliance
Lightning Source LLC
Chambersburg PA
CBHW070655050426
42451CB00008B/362